LODGE PARK

Gloucestershire

THE NATIONAL TRUST

Lodge Park is three miles east of Northleach. Approach only from A40.

Acknowledgements

Work to the building has been monitored by a small advisory panel which has met for a decade: Christopher Gibbs, representing the Trust's Arts Panel, Nicholas Cooper, representing the Architectural Panel, and Lucy Abel Smith have stayed the whole course. Their deep knowledge and infectious enthusiasm has informed and vivified what has been done. Michael Hill of Cotswold District Council and staff of English Heritage, especially Jill Kerr, the expert on historic glazing, are amongst many others who have contributed. Simon Thurley's insights into the place of coursing amongst other historic pastimes have been especially enlightening. Sir Howard Colvin provided the 1634 reference giving the earliest account of Lodge Park. The reconstruction derives from Warwick Rodwell's archaeological research, its detailing from the architect Michael Reardon, with his deep interest in Italian mannerism and Serlio, and from the builder Roger Capps, whose firm has long pioneered the revival of traditional buildings techniques.

The account of the park draws on the research of Katie Fretwell and discussion with Paul Stamper.

Jeffrey Haworth, 2001

© 2002 The National Trust
Registered charity no. 205846
ISBN 1-84359-002-6
Published by the National Trust (Enterprises) Ltd
If you would like to become a member or make a donation, please telephone 0870 458 4000; write to The National Trust, PO Box 39, Bromley, Kent BR1 3XL; or see our website at: www.nationaltrust.org.uk

Photographs: Bodleian Library, Oxford p. 25; Brian Byron pp. 6, 7, 8 (top and bottom); Conway Library, Courtauld Institute p. 27; A. C. Cooper p. 30; English Heritage/National Monuments Record p. 10; Historic Royal Palaces p. 11; National Trust pp. 5 (bottom), 12, 24, 31; National Trust Photographic Library/John Hammond pp. 4, 5 (top), 17 (top left), 21, 26, 28, 29 (top left and right and bottom left); NTPL/Nadia Mackenzie pp. 13, 16, 17 (bottom right), 18, 20, 22; NTPL/Nick Meers front cover, pp. 1, 15, 23, back cover; NTPL/Alasdair Ogilvie p. 14.

Typeset from disc and designed by James Shurmer
Print managed by Centurion Press Ltd (BAS)
for National Trust (Enterprises) Ltd,
36 Queen Anne's Gate, London SW1H 9AS

(*Front cover*) The entrance front

(*Back cover*) The balcony

(*Title-page*) The heads in the broken pediments may represent the Seven Worthies (heroic figures from history and mythology)

Bibliography

ASLET, Clive, 'Lodge Park and Sherborne House, Gloucestershire', *Country Life*, 13 March 1986, pp. 630–3.

COLVIN, Sir Howard, and others, *The History of the King's Works*, iii, iv, 1975, 1982.

MORDAUNT CROOK, J., *The Rise of the Nouveaux Riches*, 1999.

EISENTHAL, Esther, 'John Webb's Reconstruction of the Ancient House', *Architectural History*, xxviii, 1985.

FRETWELL, Katie, 'Lodge Park, Gloucestershire: A rare surviving deer course and Bridgeman layout', *Garden History*, xxiii/2, 1995, pp. 133–44.

GILBERT, Christopher, 'James Moore the Younger and William Kent at Sherborne House', *Burlington Magazine*, 1969, pp. 148–9.

GIROUARD, Mark, *Robert Smythson and the Elizabethan Country House*, 1983.

JOHNSON, Joan, *The Gloucestershire Gentry*, 1989.

WICKHAM LEGG, L. G. ed., *A Relation of a Short Survey of 26 Counties, Observed in a seven week Journey begun on 11 August, 1634 by a Captain, a Lieutenant and an Ancient*, 1904.

MIERS, Mary, 'Lodge Park, Gloucestershire', *Country Life*, 18 May 2000, pp. 82–5.

WILLOUGHBY, Leonard, 'Sherborne House, Gloucestershire', *Connoisseur*, xxx, May 1911, pp. 3–13; xxxii, February 1912, pp. 77–94.

Why not host your own event at Lodge Park?

Lodge Park's 'raison d'être' was entertainment: the Grandstand was created as an extravagant folly in which John Crump Dutton could impress his friends. To continue this tradition, it is available for hire.

The Entrance Hall, with a Cotswold stone floor, provides an ambient setting for any event when illuminated by candle light with a crackling log fire burning in the grate. Situated on the first floor is the Great Room, formerly the banqueting chamber. This light and airy setting, with windows facing north, south and east, has the benefit of double doors that open onto the balcony, affording magnificent views of the surrounding countryside. A variety of events can be accommodated in both of these areas, such as conferences, weddings and private parties. It is suitable for up to 50 people for an event such as a seated meal; up to 150 for a standing event. The Grandstand is licensed for civil weddings.

Lodge Park's appeal is enhanced by its accessibility – only one mile off the A40; 75 miles from London, 28 miles from Oxford and 12 miles from Cheltenham.

For further information and details of cost, please telephone 01451 844130.

CONTENTS

LODGE PARK

Here, uniquely, the three requirements for the ancient pastime of deer-coursing survive in one place: a park for corralling deer; a mile-long walled-in enclosure for the chase; and, overlooking its conclusion, a grandstand.

All three were created from scratch in the 1630s by John 'Crump' Dutton, a wealthy, hard-living squire with a passion for gambling. For the point of deer-coursing was to provide an opportunity for betting, and to display the abilities of different dogs.

Indeed, the Sherborne course was a public amenity, which Dutton hired out to those wanting to run their own dogs.

Today's grandstands are in the forefront of contemporary architecture, and Lodge Park was no different. Dutton was often in London as MP for Gloucestershire and was familiar with the latest trends in court architecture, modelling his grandstand on Inigo Jones's new Banqueting House.

The Lodge Park course was fully in operation by

*John 'Crump' Dutton, the builder of Lodge Park;
attributed to Franz Cleyn (Entrance Hall)*

during the following century: first, to make a smaller conventional two-storey house; then a row of three-storey cottages; and finally, in 1898, a well-designed dower-house. Unfortunately, the interior was radically simplified in 1938 by tenants and again about 1960 by Charles Dutton, 7th Lord Sherborne, who continued to inhabit Lodge Park until his death in 1982, by which time it was utterly plain and devoid of architectural interest. Without Dutton heirs in the next generation, he left the Sherborne estate to the National Trust with the wish that his housekeeper, Mrs Hall, should have the use of Lodge Park.

Encouraged by Mrs Hall, in 1991 the National Trust began to gather detailed archaeological evidence to return the grandstand to its former internal layout. For the first time in two centuries, you can now understand the original purpose and use of the building by progressing through the Hall, up the monumental staircase to the Great Room, and then again on up to the viewing platform on the roof. The basement kitchen, with the pair of great hearths and unique set of bake-ovens, has also been disinterred. The Great Room now displays the Dutton portraits and furniture made for it in 1731.

Outside, a conifer plantation and a swimming-pool have been removed from the deer-course, but the garden enclosure behind the grandstand and elements of the park beyond await restoration.

1634, when Lieutenant Hammond 'spent a full houre, with the good favour of the Keeper, in viewing that neat, rare Building, the rich furnish'd Roomes, the handsome contriv'd Pens and Places, where the Deere are kept, and turn'd out for the Course'. It continued in use for less than a century until deer-coursing was superseded by racing and fox-hunting. From the mid-1720s the landscape gardener Charles Bridgeman began remodelling the park in his angular, baroque manner for 'Crump' Dutton's great-nephew, Sir John Dutton. At the same time the grandstand was grandly modernised, apparently by William Kent. He certainly designed some of the new furniture for the Great Room, delivered in 1731.

This beautiful building, whose face is its fortune, survived neglect in the later 18th century, perhaps helped by its traditional attribution to Inigo Jones. It was disembowelled no fewer than three times

(Left) Lodge Park around 1740, when the deer-course was being used for exercising horses; detail of George Lambert's painting (Hall)

An engraving from George Turbeville's Booke of Hunting *(1576), which was still an influential guide to the subject when Lodge Park was built*

THE FIVE PHASES OF BUILDING

1 THE 17TH CENTURY

'Crump' Dutton designed Lodge Park as a viewing platform. After watching the deer-coursing from the roof, he and his guests would have descended the broad staircase to eat in the Great Room on the first floor, which was heated by the huge canopied fireplace and probably decorated with tapestries. It is this arrangement which the National Trust has partly restored. The richness of the spacious rooms used by Crump Dutton and his friends contrasts with the subterranean domain of his servants. But the staircase was conveniently placed so that food and drink could easily be carried up to the main floors from the kitchen and wine cellar.

Lieutenant Hammond's 1634 description of Lodge Park

... one stately, rich, compacted Building all of Free-stone, flat, and cover'd with Lead, with strong Battlements about not much unlike to that goodly,

1 The 17th century

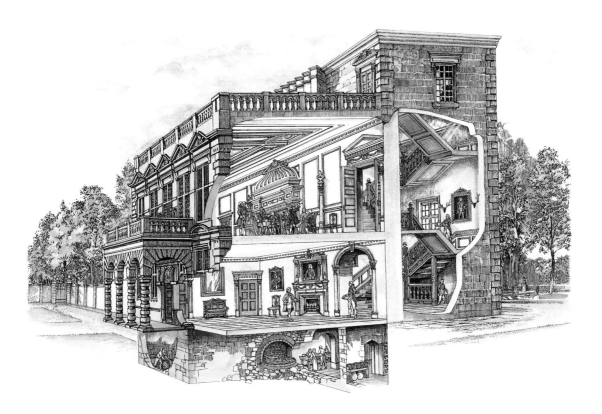

and magnificent Building the Banquetting House at Whitehall. This stately house [Mr Dutton's] is mounted on a High Hill, in the Champian, commaunding, and over-topping her owne Shire, and some neighbour Shires, adiacent, to her, plac'd with in a wall'd Parke, that is well stor'd with good Venison: This stately Lodge was lately built at the great Cost and Charges of a noble true hearted Gentleman, more for the pleasure of his worthy Friends, then his owne profit; Itt is richly furnish'd to entertaine them to see that Kingly sport, and pleasure, admirably perform'd, in that rare Paddocke course of a Mile in length, and walled on either Side. There I spent a full houre, with the good favour of the Keeper, in viewing that neat, rare Building, the rich furnish'd Roomes, the handsome contriv'd Pens and Places, where the Deere are kept, and turn'd out for the Course; and the manner, and order of the Paddock Sport.

2 THE 1720s

Sir John Dutton's account book for 1723–33 reveals the thoroughness of his stylish remodelling and refurnishing. It included new stone floors in the Porch, Hall, Staircase and Great Room. The leading stuccoist Isaac Mansfield supplied new ceiling plasterwork in the Great Room. The famous ornamental plasterer Francesco Vassalli was paid eight guineas, possibly for stucco busts.

Building work was coming to an end in October 1728, when Sir John settled with William Kent 'for his trouble making Plans for me at my Lodge and House'. Kent probably designed the new interiors as well as some of the furniture delivered in 1731.

7

3 The early 19th century

4 The mid-19th century

5 After 1898

3 THE EARLY 19TH CENTURY

Lodge Park was drastically reduced to make a small and comfortable house. The staircase and the Great Room chimneypiece were both removed, the latter to be incorporated in the rebuilding of Sherborne House by the architect Lewis Wyatt, who was a pioneer of architectural salvage.

The stability of the upper part of the building was compromised by the removal of the original flat roof structure, which acted as bracing to the walls. A conventional pitched roof was installed in an unconventional position, which trapped snow. But the front of the old stair tower, with its walled-up Jacobean doorcase, was carefully preserved.

4 THE MID-19TH CENTURY

The whole building beneath the new roof was gutted and converted into a row of cottages. The stability of the walls was further threatened by the removal of the original 17th-century first-floor framing. The ground-floor level was lowered and the new tie-beams notched for doorways to take three floors of accommodation. The unconventional lighting of the middle-floor rooms − the windows were at floor level − may have been the chief reason the cottages were apparently unoccupied by the time Augustus Hare visited Lodge Park in 1876.

5 AFTER 1898

Mr M. King of Seymour Place, London, transformed the lodge into a dower-house for Emily, wife of the 4th Lord Sherborne, in 1898–1902. The rear wing was rebuilt in a new form, and the drawing shows the first-floor front bedroom, latterly Lord Sherborne's, reduced in size for an *en suite* bathroom.

The new floor structure was at a slightly different level from the original and did not have the restraining qualities needed to anchor the walls. Beyond the ground-floor dining room was a lounge hall with a grand staircase in one corner to a first-floor drawing room. This spacious arrangement was changed to something more conventional in 1938, when the house was tenanted. Latterly, there was a small, central entrance hall with staircase beyond, drawing room to the left, and dining room on the right. This house was further simplified, when the Sherbornes took up residence in the late 1950s. When the Trust inherited the house, the external walls were moving and chimneystacks collapsing.

9

DESIGN

The design of Lodge Park is indebted to the architectural ideas that Inigo Jones was pioneering at the English court in the early 17th century; indeed, it was attributed to him for many years. Jones drew on the treatises of Italian theorists such as Sebastiano Serlio, whose *Tutte l'Opere d'Architettura et Prospettiva* (first translated into English in 1611) inspired the concept of Lodge Park and especially its intended detailing. Serlio had promoted the use of harmonic proportions for the dimensions of rooms. So the plan of the Hall is in the proportion 4:3, and its height of eleven feet is half its width. The Great Room is a double cube, a format favoured by Jones. The crowded façade owes something to the mid-16th-century pattern books of the French designers Du Cerceau and Philibert de l'Orme, while the banded columns of the loggia may derive from the work of Salomon de Brosse, as interpreted in structures such as the York House

The banded columns on the York House Watergate in London (1626–7) may have inspired those on the loggia of Lodge Park

Watergate in London. This monumental gateway, which survives near Embankment Underground station, was a prominent feature of the London riverfront in the late 1620s, when the most celebrated classical building of the period, Inigo Jones's Banqueting House, had just risen high above the Tudor turrets of Whitehall Palace. 'Crump' Dutton's lodge was ready by 1634, several years before the painted ceiling of the Banqueting House was completed.

Dutton was probably also influenced by the theatrical entertainments designed by Inigo Jones for the court of Charles I, which often exploited mythological themes. He may have thought the style appropriate for a building associated with deer, the chasing of which had a long history dating back to classical antiquity. Even the siting of Lodge Park – in the high flat windswept Cotswold landscape of unenclosed sheep runs remote from the civilised world of roads and settlements – was acknowledged architecturally. Serlio himself had associated rusticated columns of the kind that support the loggia with buildings for wild or forest places.

The general design of Lodge Park appears to emanate from an unidentified surveyor: possible candidates are Nicholas Stone, who worked for Jones on the Banqueting House (built in 1619–22), and Balthazar Gerbier, who may have designed the York House Watergate. However, the work was supervised by a master-mason – perhaps a member of the renowned Strong family of masons based nearby at Barrington. 'Crump' Dutton went to Valentine Strong in the 1650s for work to Sherborne House.

The rise of the surveyor (forerunner of the professional architect) was to devalue the inventiveness and diminish the independence of skilled artisans like the Strongs. The playwright Ben Jonson was one of those who deplored this development. In a

Inigo Jones's Banqueting House was the most famous classical building of the period

royal entertainment performed at Bolsover Castle in Derbyshire in 1634, he satirised Inigo Jones as the interfering surveyor 'Coronell Vitruvius', who puts his building workers in their place: 'Doe you know what a Surveyor is now? I tell you, a Supervisor! A hard word that, but it may be softened, and brought in to signify something. An Overseer! One that oversee-eth you. A busie man!'

At Lodge Park, however, the dominant figures still seem to have been the traditional craftsmen, who absorbed Jones's new classical style to differing degrees. So the re-creation of the interior of Lodge Park has had to take into account what we know about the attitudes of the various building trades in the early 17th century. The principal tradesmen were the mason, the fretter (plaster moulder) and the joiner:

• *The mason* was often the lead contractor in a project and often the most advanced in style. Responsible for setting out large structures, the master-mason was traditionally the master of geometry: working with divider, compass and set square, he dealt in proportional relationships rather than units of measure: classical systems of proportion would therefore present no problem.

• *Fretters* were rarer than masons and came to a site when mason and carpenter had created the carcass of a building. Moulded plaster, at least in England, is largely an innovation of the Renaissance, and the nature of the material makes it a natural vehicle for classical detail. Where the mason led, the fretter would follow, though often exhibiting a waywardness which looks odd to our eyes, using devices with which he was familiar and for which he already had moulds. It did not make for an overall integrated classical design.

• *Joiners* were even more traditional in outlook, with inherited methods of working that were inherently less amenable to expressing classical forms. Timber also lends itself to framing rather than to the mass construction which had become the chief characteristic of classical architecture. In the early 17th century the plasterer, and especially the joiner, often showed scant regard for the completed work of other trades.

RESEARCH AND REINSTATEMENT

The Sherborne Estate was accepted by the National Trust following Lord Sherborne's death in December 1982, largely because of the outstanding national importance of the Lodge Park grandstand. Its exterior had been illustrated frequently in books on English architecture as an icon of provincial Jonesian classicism. The allure of its exterior was not matched by its interior, a jumble of small-scale modern rooms and corridors, with only a stone archway and linked fireplace proclaiming an altogether nobler past.

Sir Howard Colvin's discovery of Lieutenant Hammond's 1634 description of Lodge Park (see p. 6) confirmed the suspicion that a double-cube room had once existed here. The National Trust considered reinstating this feature in a simple form, otherwise leaving the building alone – not only for its own sake, but as a place to display the Dutton portraits long in store. However, the Trust ultimately decided to reclaim the principal spaces of the original building so that visitors could better understand the way the grandstand had been used.

The work carried out by the late Nicholas Moore on the Sherborne Archive in the Gloucestershire Record Office revealed a history of dramatic alteration and refitting in the 1720s. Emily, Lady Sherborne's 1898 designs for converting Lodge Park to a dower-house were already known, but the extraordinary fact that this was the third time in the space of a century that the interior of the

The new staircase under construction

building had been entirely recast became evident only when the building archaeologist Warwick Rodwell was appointed.

In December 1990 a programme was formulated for carrying out limited archaeological investigations into the fabric of the house. The principal objectives were:

1. To examine the architectural detailing and finishes in the front part of the house, with a view to establishing their general age and significance.

2. To search for evidence relating to the form and detailing of the internal spaces in the 17th-century lodge.

3. To discover whether any features survived from William Kent's refurbishment of the property in the 1720s.

Dr Rodwell later summed up his findings:

When opening-up of the fabric began in October 1991, no features of 17th- or 18th-century date were visible except the modified dining room fireplace and adjacent arched opening. At this stage it was assumed that the lodge originally (ie in the 1630s) comprised a two-storey building of rectangular plan, with an entrance hall and service room on the ground floor, and a banqueting room which occupied the whole of the first floor. A projecting square stair turret (demolished) at the north-west corner provided access not only to the first floor, but also to the lead flat above (which served as a grandstand). Considerable doubt about the supposed simplicity of the plan had, however, been voiced by Nicholas Moore, who argued that a cellared back range had been lost.

The building is now a double-pile construction, roughly square in plan: the whole of the present back range was believed to date from *c.*1900, when the lodge was converted into a dwelling. However, investigations soon established that very little of the interior of the eastern part of the house was even as old as the conversion: many of the divisions, most of the detailing and all the finishes belonged variously to 1938 and to the mid-1960s.

Further opening-up took place, revealing that both the early history of the lodge, and the alterations of the 18th and 19th centuries, were funda-

mentally different from what had long been assumed. Most important was the realisation that the present footprint of the lodge closely reflected that of the original: the thick spine wall which divides the east and west parts was built as such, and was not the back wall of a single-pile structure. It only became an external wall in the early 19th century, when the original back range was demolished.

The second major revelation was the fact that the lodge was cellared over three-quarters of its ground floor, and that here lay a major kitchen. Parts of the cellars had been completely infilled, while other areas had been converted into a boiler house (*c.*1900) and strong-room (1960s).

Archaeological investigations continued, both during and after the vital structural repairs in 1995, yielding much evidence concerning original roof and floor levels, windows, doorways and fireplaces, as well as charting the history of alteration during the later 17th, 18th and 19th centuries.

The Great Room chimneypiece is a modern replica of the original, which was moved to Sherborne House in the early 19th century

TOUR OF THE LODGE

THE APPROACH

The armorial gateway was probably introduced in the second quarter of the 19th century – for the brief moment when Lodge Park was intended as a Dutton family residence. A possible occupant was James Dutton, the eldest son of the 2nd Lord Sherborne, but he may have left when his first wife died in 1845.

This grand entrance came into play again in the 1890s, when Emily, Lady Sherborne created a dower-house she was never to need: she predeceased her husband in 1905. She probably also built the 'tea caddy' lodges, though, rather mysteriously, a design by Mr King survives for adding the parapets: perhaps they looked too squat when first put up. The gates were linked to a large gravelled forecourt complete with circular fountain basin. The Edwardian drive between gates and house has been removed to allow the deer-course to sweep through.

The Exterior

The building was conceived as a formal front block (with the symmetrical façade facing east) and a rear block far less coherent in form. This comprised a stair tower leading up to the roof and three storeys of subsidiary rooms placed above a basement kitchen. This rear block was rebuilt in 1898–1902 and altered internally in the 1990s.

THE EAST FAÇADE

This is nearest to our ideals of classical architecture, with its symmetry and two entablatures running across as string courses, brought forward and provided with pediments at the windows. All classical windows in England had mullions and transoms until the 1660s. It says something for William Kent's admiration for Inigo Jones that such old-fashioned window openings were not replaced in the 1720s with fashionable sliding sash-windows.

The entrance gates and lodges

The east façade

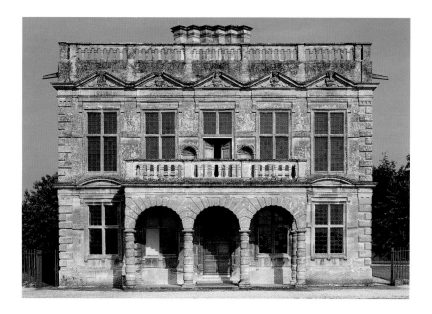

The heads in the broken pediments over the first-floor windows may represent the Seven Worthies (heroic figures from history and mythology) or portraits of people known to the masons who carved them.

The quoins at the angles of the building seem conventional enough until one looks at the top ones, which appear to be the mason's personal interpretation of Doric triglyphs as shown in Serlio's engravings.

THE LOGGIA

This handsome feature, practical both as a shelter and viewing platform, looks like an afterthought, as its mouldings collide with those of the main building, creating a visual muddle alongside the window pediments. However, archaeology confirms that the loggia was built at the same time as the rest of the grandstand.

The paving level of the loggia is original, but the slabs have been renewed, lacking the rounded mouldings of the originals, which are preserved on one surviving step and on the bases of the piers.

Half the Jacobean-style decoration around the top of the front door is thought to be a restoration. The repairs may relate to the attachment and later renewal of a pedimented timber doorcase.

The Interior

THE ENTRANCE HALL

This was planned as a robust room for crowds of people. So the floor was stone laid on the earth, this being the only part of the lodge without a cellar.

The glory of the room is the original pair of arches. One houses the fireplace with its chevron overmantel decoration into which Emily Teresa Sherborne inserted a shield with her 'ETS' monogram in 1898–1902. The heraldic fireback is dated 1784 – the year the Duttons were elevated to the peerage. The other arch, with its stone panelled soffit, leads in the grandest possible way to the staircase. The scale of the arch again indicates that this building was planned to accommodate crowds. It also explains why the left-hand window at the front of the room was originally a doorway: this feature was 'corrected' when the lodge was still new, presumably for the sake of external symmetry.

The Trust has inserted the panelled wall on the left (based on a design found at the contemporary Bolsover Castle in Derbyshire) and the pair of internal porches, which would originally have led to the servants' quarters. That on the right now leads to a room showing an introductory video about Lodge Park.

PICTURES

CLOCKWISE FROM ENTRANCE DOOR:

1 GEORGE LAMBERT (1700–65)
View of Lodge Park
Painted about 1740, following Charles Bridgeman's redesign of the park. The straight deer-course still survived, but was now being used for racing and exercising horses.

2 ENGLISH SCHOOL, c.1605–15
Captain Sir Thomas Dutton (d. 1634)
No relation of the Duttons of either Dutton or Sherborne, and indeed of altogether mysterious – but Cheshire – origin. He was knighted on the accession of James I in 1603. In 1610 he fought a duel with Sir Hatton Cheke on the beach at Calais, in which Cheke was killed. The sleeves and baggy breeches of his elaborate outfit are trimmed with silver lace. The picture was once set into a wall of the 'Vere Captains' Room at Raynham Hall in Norfolk – hence the curiously shaped frame.

3 ? After Sir ANTHONY VAN DYCK (1599–1641)
Charles I (1600–49)
The lost original may have been Van Dyck's first, still unidealised, portrait of the King.

4 After Sir ANTHONY VAN DYCK (1599–1641)
Henrietta Maria (1609–69)
Charles I's Queen.

5 By or after PAULUS MOREELSE (1571–1638)
A Shepherdess
The popularity of pastoral plays in Dutch in the 1620s and '30s gave rise to numerous pictures of this type.

6 Attributed to FRANZ CLEYN (?1582–1657/8)
John 'Crump' Dutton (1594–1656/7)
The builder of Lodge Park. Cleyn is best known for his designs for Mortlake tapestries, and for his decorative paintings in tempera at Ham House, Surrey (NT).

The Hall

Captain Sir Thomas Dutton; painted c.1605–15 (no. 2; Entrance Hall)

FURNITURE

Pair of late 17th-century English marquetry stools. Restored in 1999.

Three early 18th-century white-painted benches. Formerly heirlooms of the Evelyn family.

Mid-18th-century brass-bound chests, given to Henry Bilson-Legge (see portrait on stairs, no. 13), on his appointment as (or as a perk after being) Chancellor of the Exchequer. They were used for storing cash before the invention of cheques.

THE STAIRCASE

The staircase has been rebuilt by the Trust.

The staircase well, 18-ft square, was once even more impressive, as it originally continued up above the roof level as a tower. Apart from a small portion of the original south wall, the walls are Edwardian and thinner than the originals: rebuilding this whole tower in its first form would have been structurally unwise as well as costly.

Scarring on the west face of the spine wall showed the stairs ascended clockwise and indicated the position of the first quarter-landing. From this, the rest of the staircase could be worked out: the flights are 6 ft wide, each step having a 6½ in rise and a going of 12 in. The scale of the staircase is very large for the building, but it would have been busy with servants bringing food up from the kitchen to the Great Room. It is also paralleled by the oversize staircase at Queen Elizabeth's Hunting Lodge, Epping Forest, of the 1540s. The original staircase may have survived until the early 19th century and been removed to re-use at Sherborne House or elsewhere, but its present whereabouts are not known. The balusters of the new staircase were

The Staircase

copied directly from an external balustrade at Cornbury Park, Oxfordshire, a building exactly contemporary with Lodge Park, designed by Nicholas Stone and built by the Strong family of masons. The staircase is made of 'brown' oak from the Welsh borders, that is oak from trees that were dead some time before felling: it is immune to the yellowing effect often seen in oak joinery.

PICTURES

RIGHT OF ARCHWAY:

7 Manner of JOHN WOOTTON (?1678–1764)
Classical Landscape

FROM BOTTOM OF STAIRS:

8 Attributed to ROBERT EDGE PINE (*c.*1730–88)
The Backgammon Trio
The Duttons commissioned no fewer than three pictures of themselves playing cards or gaming. The protagonists and meaning of the present game have yet to be identified with certainty.

9 WILLIAM SARTORIUS
Greyhound and Dead Hare
Signed and dated 1731

The discovery of the signatures and dates on this and the other picture, of a spaniel, has brought to light the existence of this previously unknown member of the dynasty of painters of – chiefly – horse-portraits, from Nuremberg working and settled in England. He was probably brother to the first of them, John Sartorius (*c.*1700–*c.*1780).

10 Manner of ENOCH SEEMAN (*c.*1694–1745)
Sir John Dutton, 2nd Bt (1683/4–1742/3)
He employed William Kent and Charles Bridgeman to remodel the house and park in the 1720s and '30s.

11 After Sir ANTHONY VAN DYCK (1599–1641)
Inigo Jones (1573–1652)
Jones introduced Palladian architecture to Britain and was once thought to have designed Lodge Park.

12 After Sir GODFREY KNELLER, Bt (1646/9–1723)
John Locke (1632–1704)
The greatest English philosopher of the 17th century, and the idol of the Whigs (as Thomas Hobbes was of the Tories).

The Backgammon Trio; attributed to Robert Edge Pine (no. 8; Staircase)

13 WILLIAM HOARE of Bath (1707–92)
Rt Hon. Henry Bilson-Legge, PC, MP (1708–64)
Fourth son of the 1st Earl of Dartmouth, he had a reputation as a brilliant financier and served as Chancellor of the Exchequer in 1754–5, 1756–7 and 1757–61. He married Mary, Baroness Stawell in her own right; their granddaughter Mary married the 2nd Lord Sherborne.

14 Attributed to GEORGE KNAPTON (1698–1778)
James Lenox Naper/Dutton (1712/13–76)
Originally of Loughcrew, Meath, he inherited Sherborne, and with it Lodge Park, from his uncle, Sir John Dutton, 2nd and last Bt, in 1742/3, and consequently changed his name to Dutton.

15 ADRIAEN CARPENTIERS (active 1739–78)
Henry Bilson-Legge, 2nd Baron Stawell (1757–1820)
Signed and dated 1764
Only son of Henry Bilson-Legge (no. 13). He holds a shuttlecock and battledore (a light bat).

UPPER LANDING:

35 *The Articles and Orders of the Paddock Course at Sherborne in Gloucestershire*
See p. 32.

36 Manner of Sir PETER LELY (1618–80)
A Young Girl

37 DANIEL GARDNER (*c.*1750–1805)
Henry Bilson-Legge, 2nd Baron Stawell (1757–1820)
An adult portrait of the boy on the stairs. In 1779, probably around the time that this gouache was painted, he married the Hon. Mary Curzon, daughter of the 1st Viscount Curzon. They only had a daughter (also Mary, who married the 2nd Baron), so the title died with him.

38 WILLIAM SARTORIUS
Black Water Spaniel with a dead Duck
Signed and dated 1731

THE GREAT ROOM

This strikingly advanced classical room is the counterpart to the ambitious exterior of Lodge Park. Here 'Crump' Dutton would have entertained his guests, who could view the deer-course from the balcony or by climbing the stairs to the roof.

RESTORATION

What has been recovered in the 1990s is inevitably an inadequate substitute for what was destroyed two centuries ago. However, though precise detail is known only for the fireplace, archaeological investigation has established fixed points, such as the exact floor and ceiling levels, the dimensions of the classical entablature, and the height of the ceiling cove. Evidence also allowed for the fixing of dado panelling and for architraves and panelled reveals to all the windows.

The new work aims to re-establish the form of the room and hint at some of its detail: thus the entablature follows that on the outside of the building, which is the same size, and the pilaster capitals relate to those next to the front door. The work does not go much beyond restoring the classical ordering of the room, with dado, pilaster and entablature. Joinery and plasterwork may once have been far more elaborate, with much of the woodwork painted, grained or marbled and enriched with colour and gilding. The plain plaster walls would almost certainly have been hung with tapestry to give the 'rich furnish'd' effect recorded by Lieutenant Hammond in 1634. Lacking that, they instead allowed the hanging of the portraits that formerly hung in Sherborne House.

Though the formidable floor structure for this room has been re-created, with a cat's cradle of beams, sub-beams and joists, the appearance of the original floor surface is unknown. The opportunity has been taken to use spectacular 49 ft (15 m) long, tapered boards from chestnuts felled on the Welsh border. However, the floor may originally have been stone slabs – the material with which Sir John Dutton paved the room in the 1720s, when it became his dining room.

CHIMNEYPIECE

The chimneypiece is a spirited modern version by masons of the Hereford Cathedral Workshop of the original, which was moved in the early 19th century to the Horse Parlour at Sherborne House. Even though Sherborne is now divided into 35 flats and the chimneypiece is now in a cupboard, English Heritage would not allow its return to Lodge Park. This colossal, continental form of chimneypiece is little known in England except at

The Great Room

Bolsover Castle. However, there is a small group of them in Gloucestershire – at Upper Swell Manor, that formerly at Lodge Park, and an even larger one always in the Great Hall at Sherborne House.

PAINTED GLASS

The painted glass includes the Dutton arms (in window right of entrance door).

PICTURES

SOUTH (FAR) WALL:

27 ENGLISH SCHOOL, 1690S
Mary Barwick, Lady Dutton (d. 1721/3)
She was married to Sir Ralph Dutton, 1st Bt, in 1678/9, as his secon.5d wife, and bore him seven children, including the 2nd and last Baronet, and Anne, who married James Naper, and was thus grandmother of the 1st Baron Sherborne.

28 18th-century copy of Sir ANTHONY VAN DYCK (1599–1641)
Thomas Wentworth, 1st Earl of Strafford (1593–1641)
Charles I's efficient, but widely hated, chief minister. He was impeached for treason by Parliament and executed when the King abandoned him.

29 Manner of Sir GODFREY KNELLER, Bt (1646/9–1723)
Mary Dutton, Lady Reade (d. 1721)
Sister of Sir John Dutton, 2nd Bt. She was married in 1719 to Sir Thomas Reade, 4th Bt, MP (*c.*1683–1752), of Shipton Court, Shipton-under-Wychwood, Oxfordshire, but died two years later, a week after giving birth to the future 6th Baronet.

30 ENGLISH SCHOOL, *c.*1660
Dr John Barwick (1612–64)
Elder brother of Peter Barwick (see no. 31), who supported him in his efforts to further the Royalist cause during the Civil War and the Commonwealth. He was imprisoned in the Tower of

London for treason in 1650 by Parliament, but released without trial two years later, in much better health, thanks to an enforced diet of fruit and water. He became the clearing-house for secret correspondence with the exiled Charles II, who appointed him Dean of St Paul's in 1661.

CHIMNEYPIECE WALL:

21 Sir PETER LELY (1618–80)
Supposed Portrait of Frances Cromwell
(1638–1720/1)
The youngest daughter of Oliver Cromwell. 'Crump' Dutton's will expressed the wish to Cromwell that he should become the guardian of his nephew, William Dutton, and that, 'according to the discourse that hath passed between us', she should marry William. Instead, however, she married Robert Rich, grandson of the Cromwellian admiral, Robert, 2nd Earl of Warwick. This may, however, really be a portrait of the Hon. Mary Scudamore/Russell, whom William Dutton married instead.

Dr Peter and Mrs Barwick and their daughter Mary, who married Sir Ralph Dutton, 1st Bt; by Jacob Huysmans (no. 34; Great Room)

22 ENGLISH SCHOOL, early 19th-century
William Dutton (before 1640–74/5)
Nephew and heir of 'Crump' Dutton. This picture would appear to have been painted as a pendant to the supposed portrait of Frances Cromwell, so as to have images of both protagonists of the would-be alliance.

23 SAMUEL BROWNE (active c.1680–c.1691)
Sir Ralph Dutton, 1st Bt (d. 1720/1)
He inherited Lodge Park from his uncle, 'Crump' Dutton, whose passion for gambling he shared.

24 Manner of SIR GODFREY KNELLER, Bt
(1646/9–1723)
Mary Barwick, Lady Dutton (d. 1721/3)
Recent cleaning revealed the inscription, which identifies this as Sir Ralph Dutton's second wife (see no. 27).

25 ENGLISH SCHOOL, late 18th-century
? Sir Ralph Dutton (d. 1720/1) *as a Boy*
This seems to have been painted as a pendant to the portrait of his future wife (no. 24).

26 After FRANZ CLEYN (?1582–1657/8)
John 'Crump' Dutton (1594–1656/7)
An enlarged version of the head-and-shoulders portrait in the Hall, probably painted after his death.

NORTH (NEAR WALL):

16 Manner of Sir ANTHONY VAN DYCK
(1599–1641)
A Lady in Blue

17 ENGLISH SCHOOL, c.1650
An Unknown Man, called Sir Thomas Browne
(1605–82)
The supposed subject of this portrait was author of *Religio Medici* (1642), one of the most idiosyncratic and compelling books in English literature, and of *Urn Burial* (1658), the first archaeological treatise in English. His mother remarried Sir Thomas Dutton, which may explain why the Duttons of Sherborne later acquired this spurious portrait.

18 ENGLISH SCHOOL, c.1650
An Unknown Man, called Thomas Dutton
(1506/7–81) *of Chester*
The supposed sitter was the second son of William Dutton of Dutton; he bought the manor of Sherborne in 1551, but it was his grandson, John 'Crump' Dutton, who first made it his seat. This picture, however, dates from a century later.

19 MICHAEL DAHL (1656/9–1743)
Mary Cullen, Lady Dutton (d. 1719)
Labelled as Grizel Poole, Mrs Dutton, first wife of Sir Ralph Dutton, 1st Bt, who died in 1677, but, from its likely date, probably really Mary Cullen, who married Sir John Dutton, 2nd Bt, in 1714. Her father, Sir Rushout Cullen, built Upton House, Warwickshire (NT), in the 1690s.

20 Manner of Sir ANTHONY VAN DYCK
(1599–1641)
Imaginary Portrait of 'Old' William Dutton
(1561–1618)
The father of 'Crump' Dutton. This picture dates from the mid-17th century and is by the same hand as that of his son (no.26), to the right of the chimneypiece.

BALCONY WALL:

31 JACOB HUYSMANS (c.1633–c.1696)
Dr Peter Barwick (1619–1705)
Younger brother of Dr John Barwick, whose life he wrote in Latin (1721; transl. 1724), and a wealthy physician to Charles II. A Royalist and devout churchman like his brother, he stayed in London throughout the Great Plague (1665) and gave free medical consultations to the poor. His daughter married Sir Ralph Dutton, 1st Bt.

32 MICHAEL DAHL (1656/9–1743)
A Daughter of William, 1st Earl of Dartmouth
Either Lady Barbara, Lady Bagot (d. 1765), or Lady Anne, Lady Holte (1720–40). Their brother was Henry Bilson-Legge (see no. 13).

33 Attributed to JOHN HAYLS (active 1651–79)
'Mrs Hoare'
As yet unidentified.

34 JACOB HUYSMANS (c.1633–c.1696)
Dr Peter and Mrs Barwick and their daughter Mary
For Peter Barwick, see above. Around 1657 he married Mrs Sayon, a merchant's widow, and a kinswoman of the judicially murdered Archbishop Laud. Their daughter, Mary, was the second wife of Sir Ralph Dutton, 1st Bt.

FURNITURE

Pair of mahogany benches, made for this room in 1731 by James Moore the Younger to a design by William Kent (on loan from Temple Newsam, Leeds). Documented Kent furniture is very rare.

Two of the four side-tables were also made by Moore for this room in the 1730s. Those against the fireplace wall have lost their original marble tops and gilding, although flecks of gold leaf are still visible on the stands.

Set of six late 17th-century high-backed chairs.

Walk out on to the balcony to enjoy the view of the deer-course. Leave the Great Room by the door you entered, turn left on the landing, and take the spiral staircase to the roof.

The mahogany benches were made for the Great Room in 1731 by James Moore the Younger to a design by William Kent (on loan from Temple Newsam)

The roof platform

THE TURRET STAIR AND ROOF PLATFORM

The spiral staircase rises over the Edwardian wing to a cupola which has been made to look Edwardian rather than 17th-century so that visitors do not mistake it for an original feature. The 17th-century splat balusters guarding the top of the stairs are from the staircase in the long-demolished service wing at Croft Castle in Herefordshire. These have been copied for the external platform leading to the main roof.

Before the trees grew up, there would have been a good view of most of the deer-course, especially straight ahead where the race reached its climax. Beyond, the desolate, unenclosed high Cotswold landscape would have seemed forbidding and potentially dangerous in sharp contrast to the conviviality at the Lodge. Though there is original bench seating in the stonework beyond the chimneystacks, the view to the park behind was not important. Indeed, it was largely hidden by the chimneys and by the original stair tower.

The chimney shafts are only 3 in (7.5 cm) thick and not joined to each other except at the top. Repairs in 1995 prevented imminent collapse.

The stonework of the balustrade was even more eroded, but great care has been taken to retain each piece of sound stone. Miniature arcading was often used as an alternative to balusters in the early 17th century, both externally and especially for internal staircases.

Walk back down the stairs and descend to the basement.

THE CELLAR KITCHEN

Directly opposite the steps to the cellar, you can see the serving hatch. Food would have been prepared in the kitchen by one set of servants, sweaty from the heat, and then passed through this hatch to another set of clean, well-dressed servants, who would have carried it upstairs.

With labour cheap and Sherborne House two miles away, a substantial kitchen was both affordable and necessary. The major surprise in excavating the room was to discover such elaborate arrangements for baking: the set of three ovens is a very remarkable survival.

The kitchen would have had an outside door at the far end of the room and been lit by windows, now lost, along the side. A lockable storeroom for food or wine survives at the bottom of the main stairs.

THE PARK AND DEER-COURSING AT LODGE PARK

Before 'Crump' Dutton, there was already a park at Sherborne north of the River Windrush, which had been walled for deer in the late 16th century. For an old park, it occupies a surprisingly fertile site. Typically, the manor house, Sherborne House, stands outside this park, to the south, but the old park was made visually one with the surroundings of the mansion by 18th-century landscaping. By the mid-19th century, several hundred acres of additional parkland had been created as far south as the present A40. Subsequent straightening of this road has left the Cheltenham Lodges with their splendid iron gates, all of c.1840, magnificently isolated beyond the vast semicircle of greensward.

LODGE PARK

'Crump' Dutton set about enclosing his 'New Park' out of agriculturally worthless wasteland soon after he inherited Sherborne in 1618. By the 1620s he was acquiring parcels of land, and by 1634 it was ready for deer-coursing. A warrant dated 1655 and

signed by Oliver Cromwell allowed Dutton to take bucks and roes from Wychwood Forest for this new park. The following year Dutton was dead.

Lodge Park was unusual in having a purpose-built course and a permanent grandstand; most were temporary affairs constructed from hurdles within an existing park. Records of permanent deer-courses are very scarce, though one existed at Badminton into the 18th century. Another is shown on a 1699 map at Bramshill in Hampshire, while a royal example existed at Hampton Court, with walls built in 1537 by Henry VIII, a leading promoter of deer-coursing. The Hampton course was similar to Lodge Park with its walled mile-long extent and a building serving as a grandstand at one end. By the 1690s it had been landscaped away.

The inclusion of instructions for deer- or paddock-coursing in manuals such as Turberville's *Booke of Hunting* (1576) and Blome's *The Gentleman's Recreation* (1686) suggests that the sport was popular until about 1700. Since Sir John Dutton's landscape improvements (up to his death in 1742/3) appear to have been designed partly to help in corralling deer, the 'sport' may have carried on longer at Sherborne than elsewhere.

THE SHERBORNE DEER-COURSE AND ITS OPERATION

The mile-long course seems to have been standard and ran from the present A40 to just past the grandstand. The course was slightly funnel-shaped, about 219 yd (200 m) wide at the start to 98 yd (90 m) at the grandstand end, and enclosed by 6½ ft (2 m) high walls.

(Left) A stag, illustrated in Turbeville's Booke of Hunting *(1576)*

Charles Bridgeman's 1729 plan of the park (Gough drawings a4 fol. 68r, Bodleian Library, Oxford)

The handwritten *Articles and Orders of the Paddock Course at Sherborne in Gloucestershire*, which was probably compiled in the 18th century from published manuals (see p. 32), notes two types of race: a 'breathing course', which was more commonly run; and, for much higher stakes and fees, a 'fleshing course', when presumably the deer could be killed. As the architectural historian Simon Thurley has

observed, the point of most sports – then as now – was as a medium for betting. First, the dogs were slipped from their collars by a 'slipper'. The finishing post – a narrow ditch – was in front of the grandstand so that it was clear which dog was nearest to the deer and therefore who had won the wager. At the end of the race, the deer (usually fallow) jumped over a wide ditch where the dogs could not follow, being caught and led away where the walled enclosure greatly narrows to the south. There are further rules about the use of a terrier or 'teazer', 'a sort of mongrel greyhound' that drove the deer down the course before the dogs were slipped, as well as about what was to happen if the deer did not run straight.

SIR JOHN DUTTON'S IMPROVEMENTS

In 1709 John Dutton was handed the estate and debts of his father, Ralph, sportsman, gambler and spendthrift. John's more economical management allowed him to improve his property using leading designers. To redesign the park, in 1726 he engaged Charles Bridgeman, the greatest landscaper of the day and at that time working on the vast gardens at Stowe in Buckinghamshire. Dutton's accounts record two visits by Bridgeman, once in 1725 and again in 1729, when he was paid £70 for his services and for supplying 'a plan for my New Park'. It is not known whether this was the plan attached to Sir John's Will, in which he stipulated that the design was to be finished by his heir (payments confirm this was done). But it was probably similar to a plan recently found in a collection of Bridgeman's drawings in the Bodleian Library, Oxford, by David Jacques, Chairman of the Garden History Society. It shows a series of immense 'outdoor

rooms' (presumably for herding deer), a 'Great Avenue', aligned on a feature behind the Lodge, together with a serpentine canal. In 1733 high walls were built either side of the lodge. A stone terrace was made behind, and a ha-ha dug in 1735 to separate the small wilderness garden from the park. In 1730 more work was carried out on the forecourt of the lodge, including adding 'Rustick Pilasters' on the walls flanking the building. The Kent-style gateway next to the Edwardian coach-house was probably added in 1740.

Many trees were purchased – the accounts record 10,000 Scots pines, 800 willows and 4,500 hawthorn. In 1735 and 1736 over 4,600 tree holes were dug, probably mainly in plantations enclosed by hawthorn hedges. The finished park is shown in George Lambert's bird's-eye view, and there were deer in the park for nearly two centuries after that.

A survey made a century later reveals that the Great Avenue and the canal had gone, but that much of the design shown in the Bodleian plan survived, though heavily eroded. There has been further erosion since then. Even so, Lodge Park is one of the very few surviving designs by Bridgeman not to have been overlaid by the work of the better-remembered designers, William Kent and 'Capability' Brown.

The park in the 1740s, as painted by George Lambert

THE DUTTONS

Thomas Dutton (1506/7–81), the younger son of an obscure Cheshire squire who rose to become Crown Surveyor of Gloucestershire, bought the manor of Sherborne in 1551.

Thomas's son, William (1561–1618), was High Sheriff in 1590 and 1601 and Deputy Lieutenant for Gloucestershire. His marriage to the daughter of a Lord Mayor of London may have helped finance his property-buying, which included the seven-square-mile estate of Standish eight miles south of Gloucester. Tradition has it that he could ride from Sherborne to Cheltenham sixteen miles away entirely on his own land.

JOHN 'CRUMP' DUTTON
(1594–1656/7)

William's son John had all the advantages of money and land, but his personal tragedy was his deformity: he was hunch-backed. Even so, he lived life to the full and was a determined gambler. Hence his introduction of deer-coursing at Sherborne, one of the most expensive, and therefore prestigious, opportunities for gambling.

According to the strongest of the family traditions, he was fond of gambling recklessly with friends at a small inn near Sherborne. On one occasion, having lost heavily, he suddenly offered to stake Sherborne itself. The cry immediately went out, 'Sherborne is up!' His faithful butler overheard the shout, and realising instantly what a rash act this was, he rushed into the room, picked up his master in his arms, and carried him home on horseback, still kicking and struggling. Thus was Sherborne saved. By contrast, the 17th-century antiquary Anthony Wood speaks of him as being 'a learned

and prudent man, and as one of the richest, so one of the meekest men in England'.

Dutton steered a complicated course through the dangerous waters of Civil War England. He seems to have started out as a moderate Parliamentarian and was twice returned to Parliament from Gloucester Gaol, where he had been sent for refusing to collect the King's hated Ship Money tax from his neighbours. He then became a Royalist, helping to organise the defence of Oxford, and

(Right) 'Crump' Dutton's tomb in Sherborne church

was fined £6,000 by Parliament. After the King's execution in 1649, he resumed an earlier friendship with Oliver Cromwell, making Cromwell guardian of his nephew and heir, William Dutton, with the expressed desire that William would marry Cromwell's youngest daughter Frances. Crump excluded his daughters from succession at Sherborne because they had married steadfast Royalists. In the event, William succeeded to Sherborne only after a long lawsuit and never married Cromwell's daughter. He had no surviving children and so Sherborne passed to his brother, Sir Ralph Dutton, MP.

SIR RALPH DUTTON, 1ST BARONET (d. 1720/1)

Sir Ralph bred greyhounds and gambled heavily on them. In the 1690s he was the acknowledged expert on deer-coursing in the south of England. His second marriage was to a daughter of the wealthy

Sir Ralph Dutton, 1st Bt, who inherited Lodge Park from his uncle, 'Crump' Dutton; by Samuel Browne (no. 23; Great Room)

physician to Charles II, Dr Peter Barwick. Dutton received £10,000 on the marriage, and Dr Barwick saved him from financial scrapes. No wonder Dr Barwick's Will speaks bitterly of Dutton. Sir Ralph was eventually reduced to living on an allowance of £400 a year, handing over his estate and debts to his son in 1709.

SIR JOHN DUTTON, 2ND AND LAST BARONET (1683/4–1742/3)

John Dutton was energetic, kind, sensible and retiring. He ran the estate carefully, keeping detailed accounts and gradually paying off his father's debts. Besides making extensive improvements at Sherborne House and Lodge Park, which became possible when the estate was back in good heart, he bought William Kent's *Works of Inigo Jones*, James Gibbs's *Designs in Architecture* and works by Swift and Pope. He also looked at other houses and gardens. His lively interest in developments in architecture and landscaping led him to employ both William Kent and Charles Bridgeman as well as the best craftsmen of the day, including James Moore the Younger, who supplied '2 Mahogany settees for ye Dining Room at ye Lodge carved £30' in 1731 (which have been lent back to Lodge Park by Temple Newsam, Leeds). Moore also made '4 Mahogany Stools Carved for ye Dining Room at ye Lodge £20', which match the settees. Two of them have recently been export-stopped in Canada, preventing their return to Britain.

Sir John married two heiresses: Mary Cullen, whose father built Upton House, Banbury, brought him £12,500; and Mary Keck of Great Tew, who brought him £20,000. But there were to be no children to inherit, and so the estate passed to his nephew by marriage, James Naper, who took the surname Dutton in 1748.

(Right) James Lenox Naper, who changed his name to Dutton in 1748 after inheriting the Sherborne estate from his uncle; attributed to George Knapton (no. 14; Staircase)

Sir John Dutton, 2nd Bt, who employed William Kent and Charles Bridgeman to remodel the house and park in the 1730s and '40s; manner of Enoch Seeman (no. 10; Staircase)

John, 2nd Lord Sherborne, who inherited in 1820 and transformed the estate over the next 42 years

THE SHERBORNES

In 1784 James's son, another James, was created 1st Baron Sherborne, but seems to have made few changes. The 2nd Baron Sherborne inherited in 1820 and in the following 42 years transformed his inheritance, building cottages by the dozen, rebuilding Sherborne church and in the late 1820s employing Lewis Wyatt to reconstruct Sherborne House – a drawn-out affair because the clerk-of-works neglected his duties, and dry rot broke out; Anthony Salvin took over as architect. The antiquarian-minded Wyatt may have been responsible for saving Lodge Park from demolition by reducing it to a small house, and at the same time removing the great chimneypiece from the Great Room as an ornament for the new Sherborne House.

The inveterate country-house visitor Augustus Hare was shown round Lodge Park in 1876: 'This afternoon I have been with Miss Dutton and charming Miss Ruth Bouverie to the old chase and the deer-park, in which there is a beautiful deserted hunting lodge by Inigo Jones. Lady Sherborne wanted to make a garden in front of it, but was only allowed by her lord to have grass instead of potatoes.'

The 4th Baron inherited in 1883. His main interests were birds and history: books on ornithology displaced works by Voltaire and Rousseau in the Sherborne library; and his great archive was catalogued and properly stored. But most of all, he kept his property in the peak of condition.

Emily, Lady Sherborne, who restored Lodge Park as a dower-house for herself in 1898–1902, but died before she could move in

He married late in life Emily, daughter of the immensely rich Baron de Stern. Expecting that she would survive him, she converted Lodge Park into a dower-house for herself from her own purse. It was finished in 1902, but she died in 1905, presumably never having lived there. He survived the First World War, dying in 1919. His surviving brother, also childless, died in 1920, leaving their nephew James Huntley Dutton to succeed as 6th Baron. When he died in 1949, he had only a few hundred pounds to leave each of his four children; Sherborne House had been given up many years before.

CHARLES DUTTON, 7TH BARON SHERBORNE (1911–82)

Not only was Charles Sherborne virtually penniless, but he had also lost an arm to TB. His proudest achievement was to learn to fly despite this disability, which he hated and embarrassed him throughout the rest of his life. Occasionally, the old deer-course would make an ideal airfield. During the Second World War he made a very happy marriage to Joan, the daughter of the Canadian multi-millionnaire Sir James Hamet Dunn. Sir James died in the late 1950s, leaving his daughter £2 million.

'When the money came', the Sherbornes moved into Lodge Park and laid down an extensive cellar in preparation for a lifestyle to match their new fortune. Finding it difficult to get staff, they took on Major Ralph Moore-Stevens as gardener-mechanic and his wife Betty as cook-housekeeper so long as they remembered to say 'lordship' and 'ladyship' once each morning. This extraordinary friend-servant relationship worked remarkably well until Major Moore-Stevens died in 1973. At this point, according to Betty, Lord Sherborne instructed her, 'You had better marry Bill', who was an excellent mechanic from one of the village families. Betty was even more surprised when, after Lady Sherborne had died in 1982, Lord Sherborne said, 'Betty, you had better divorce Bill and marry me'. This time she refused, but nevertheless he left her the tenancy of Lodge Park for her lifetime.

The Sherbornes were both tall and elegant and

The 7th Lord Sherborne's dining room at Lodge Park

made a striking couple on the rare occasions they were seen in public. Charles Sherborne might often be found racing at Cheltenham, but they led a very private life, hardly seen by their tenants. At Lodge Park Lady Sherborne planted a thuja hedge which shielded much of the forecourt from public view, and spent most of her time in a cheap off-the-peg summer-house close to the house in a small enclosure inhabited by ornamental fowl. Another enclosure nearer the road housed an equally private swimming-pool.

When Lord Sherborne asked one day, 'Who is the man I have found in the passage?', Betty replied, 'He is your estate foreman. He has worked for you five years.' His lack of interest in day-to-day matters must have made it much easier for his professional agent to manage the estate: the 1960s saw proper drainage and bathrooms installed throughout Sherborne village, and the cottages were put into basic repair.

The Sherbornes held a constant round of lunch and dinner parties for a restricted circle of friends and relations. Betty did most of the shopping, cooking and clearing away, and her energy seems to have kept the show on the road. When she over-stepped the mark, Lady Sherborne would sack her, and then promptly reinstate her.

One morning, Lord and Lady Sherborne discovered six Rolls-Royces from the London car dealer Jack Barclay, all different colours, circling the forecourt. Each denied that they had ordered the cars. Eventually they shouted in concert, 'It was you, Betty, and you must choose the colour.' 'And', added Lady Sherborne, 'you must stop a pint of milk a day to make up for this extravagance.'

In the short interval between Lady Sherborne's death and his own in 1982, Lord Sherborne had thought about the future of an estate that had belonged to his family for more than four centuries. Following a prompt from his Land Agent, he left Sherborne to the National Trust with the wish that it would be kept together as a traditional Cotswold estate.

The atmosphere of fun and unreality persisted at Lodge Park until Bill and Betty, who had cancer, moved to an easier life in the coach-house in 1992. No more would Betty say, 'Crump is cross. I heard him clumping down the stairs last night' or, suddenly, when deep in discussion, 'Look over there, it's Crumpy'.

APPENDIX
The Articles and Orders of the Paddock Course at Sherborne in Gloucestershire

Imprimis;

It is agreed upon that the keeper shall put up his Deer at a days warning for any Gentleman to run his Dogs paying his Fees which is half a Crown a Dog and twelve pence to the Slipper for a breathing Course.

Item,

If any match be made of Twenty Pounds a Dog they are to have a Fleshing Course of each side paying the Fee which is Ten Shillings a Deer.

Item,

That the Deer must run at Post Law and no less without the consent of the keepers.

Item,

If the Deer do turn again before He cometh to the Pinching Post; that Match is to be run again, giving an hours space.

Item,

If any Dog do Pinch before he come to the Pinching Post, winneth the Match, and if neither of the Dogs do Pinch, then that Dog which first leapeth the Ditch winneth the Match.

Item,

That the Dogs shall be brought in the Dog-slips at the Hour appointed according to the Articles drawn betwixt them.

Item,

If one Dog do come at the hour appointed, and not the other, then that which doth come is to run at a breathed Deer down the Course and the other to pay the forfeiture according to the Articles.

Item,

If anyone of the Dogs which is to run a match do break his Collar before he cometh to be fair slipped; that Dog is to run again within the space of two hours at the farthest, and the former to be no match in case the other be slipped, but if the other be not slipped, then the Match to be run again the third day after.

Item,

That no Match be run in Frost or Snow but shall be put off from three days to three days till the Weather do serve as the Parties shall think fit.

Item,

That the Keeper shall slip the Dogs with falling Collars.

Item,

That before the Dogs be put in the slip, the Judges shall be at the Ditch appointed, and at the Pinching Post, and to be made a match but by the Judges.

Item,

If any match be run for above Five Pounds, the Keeper is to have Twelve pence in the Pound.

Item,

That He that keepeth the Stakes shall pay the Keeper before he delivereth the Stakes.

Item,

That if He that hath the better of that match where the Deer turns again or where the Deer is killed before he comes to the Pinching Post doth not require the other to run it again before he goeth out of the Field, the Course shall be at an End, and not to be run any more. But if he require it then; it must be run that Day.

Item,

If the Deer do turn or swerve after he is past the Pinch Post, in so much that at the time of the turning or swerving, the Head of the Deer is more towards the Pen from whence he came, than to the Pen whither he is going; Then that Dog that is nearest the Deer at the time of the said turning or swerving winneth the match.